Awesome Facts about

Tornadoes

This edition published in 2001
© Aladdin Books Ltd 1998
Produced by
Aladdin Books Ltd
28 Percy Street
London W1P 0LD

ISBN 0-7496-4244-0 (paperback)

Previously published in hardcover
in the series 'I Didn't Know That'
ISBN 0-7496-3113-9 (hardback)

First published in Great Britain in 1998 by
Aladdin Books/Watts Books
96 Leonard Street
London EC2A 4XD

Editor: Liz White
Design: David West Children's Books
Illustrators: Peter Roberts, Jo Moore

Printed in the U.A.E.

Awesome Facts
about
Tornadoes

Kate Petty

Aladdin / Watts
London • Sydney

Contents

Introduction

Did *you* know that dust devils can be a kilometre high? ... that hurricanes can pile up boats like bath toys? ... that it can rain frogs, fish and schoolchildren?

Discover for yourself amazing facts about violent weather, from the hailstone as big as a tennis ball (but much heavier!) to the storm surge that can fling boats a kilometre inland.

Look out for this symbol which means there is a fun project for you to try.

Is it true or is it false? Watch for this symbol and try to answer the question before reading on for the answer.

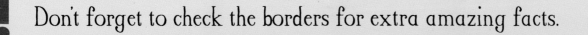

Don't forget to check the borders for extra amazing facts.

Cloudy memories

The weather is a powerful force. William Rankin realised this when he bailed out of his plane in a violent thunderstorm. He was bounced around in the clouds, buffeted by the wind, for a terrifying 45 minutes before finally parachuting to safety.

In 1876, Denonath Sircar of Bangladesh clung to a broken branch all night to save himself in floods that washed away millions of homes.

The terrible hurricane that hit the Caribbean in 1780 killed 20,000 people. The wind was so violent that it hurled a six-kilogram cannon 128 metres.

In 1931, a Minnesota tornado tossed a railway carriage 25 m through the air.

Deanna Wyant and her boyfriend actually flew around the room when a tornado hit their apartment in 1965. The building collapsed but miraculously they both survived!

Storm brewing

A thunderhead is the very top of a stormcloud. Some thunderheads can be over 15 km high. The name for a thundercloud is cumulonimbus. Cumulus means 'heaped' and nimbus means 'raincloud'. You can see fluffy, low-level cumulus clouds building up into tall thunderclouds in warm weather.

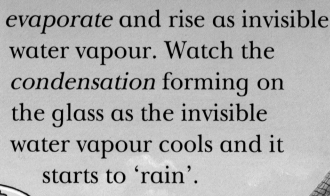

Leave an upturned jar on a saucer of water in a sunny spot for an hour. The heat of the sun will cause some of the water to *evaporate* and rise as invisible water vapour. Watch the *condensation* forming on the glass as the invisible water vapour cools and it starts to 'rain'.

Cold air

Warm air

Clouds can be formed in many ways. In this case a mass of warm moist air moves in from the right. It rises over the cold air mass moving in from the left. Rain falls where the two masses meet.

3 The base of the cloud is low. The top is very high.

2 The air cools as it gets higher and droplets form.

1 In hot weather warm wet air and dust rise to form cumulus clouds.

 Around the Equator there are about 30,000 thunderstorms every day.

ONE AND TWO AND THREE AND

Thunderstruck

Thunder is the sound of lightning. The moving air inside a thundercloud builds up *static electricity*. This causes a huge flash of lightning which heats the air to 30,000°C. The air expands and explodes, making a thunderclap.

How far away is the storm? Count the seconds between the time when you see the lightning and the time when you hear the thunder. Count one kilometre for every three seconds.

Don't try Benjamin Franklin's famous 1752 experiment with a kite and a key to prove the electrical nature of lightning. A Swedish scientist, trying it out for himself in 1909, was electrocuted.

Reports of 'ball lightning' have not been scientifically proved. A ball of lightning supposedly floated around a hotel room in France before drifting out of the window and exploding nearby.

In 1894, a hailstone that landed in the USA contained a frozen turtle.

True or false?
Firing shells at clouds can prevent hailstorms.

Answer: **True**

Anti-hail gunners in Uzbekistan fire shells, scattering tiny particles into the clouds. The smaller hailstones that cling to them melt before reaching the ground.

The largest hailstones fell during a storm in Bangladesh that killed 92 people in 1986. Each hailstone weighed 1 kg.

Huge hailstones

Sometimes *hailstones* can be as big as tennis balls! In India, these huge hailstones smashed car windscreens, flattened crops and killed thousands of birds. Many farmers now insure themselves against hail damage.

SEARCH & FIND & FIND & SEARCH

Can you find the fish?

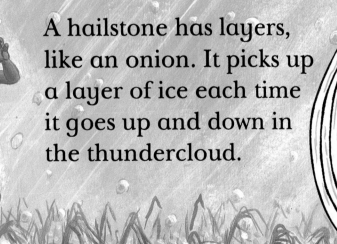

A hailstone has layers, like an onion. It picks up a layer of ice each time it goes up and down in the thundercloud.

Blizzard behaviour

Can you find the rucksack?

SEARCH & FIND SEARCH & FIND

Blizzards are severe snowstorms. To survive in one you should lie down. The blanket of snow traps a layer of warm air around the body. Remember to make an airhole! Animals often survive in the snow this way.

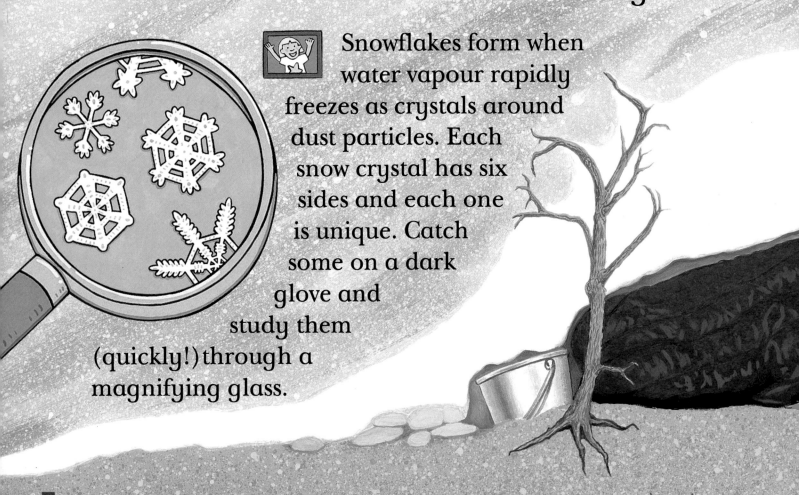

Snowflakes form when water vapour rapidly freezes as crystals around dust particles. Each snow crystal has six sides and each one is unique. Catch some on a dark glove and study them (quickly!) through a magnifying glass.

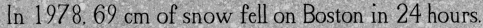

In 1978, 69 cm of snow fell on Boston in 24 hours.

Avalanche! A weakness in a layer of snow on a slope or a precipice can start an avalanche. As thousands of tonnes of snow roars downhill it can reach speeds of over 300 km/h, burying everything in its path.

St Bernard dogs were first kept by monks in the Swiss mountains to rescue people trapped in the snow. They wore barrels of brandy for reviving the patients.

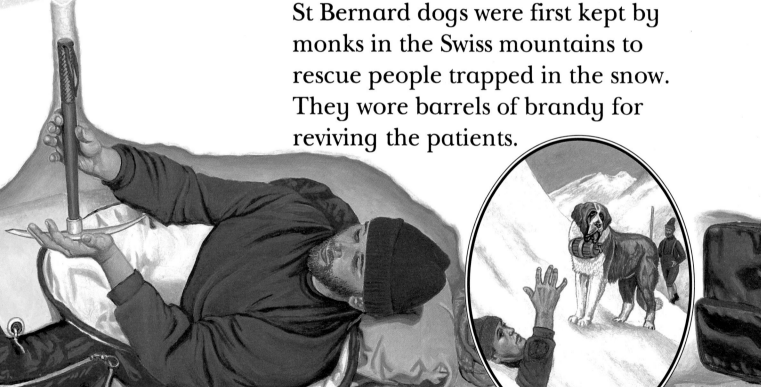

Monster monsoons

Monsoons are rainstorms which can last for up to six months. Water from the Indian Ocean evaporates in the winter and then falls as torrential rain in the summer monsoons. Farmers in low-lying parts of India can lose everything. In July, Mumbai (Bombay) has eight times as much rain as New York City!

Showers of frogs have occurred in many places such as India and England! Other showers include crabs, fish and jellyfish.

Land is flooded when rain makes a river rise over its banks. Noah's flood is based on fact. There were floods in the Tigris-Euphrates valley in Turkey and Mesopotamia around 4000 BC.

You can make your own rain gauge from a flat-bottomed plastic bottle. Find out how much rain falls in one month where you live.

Top of plastic bottle is cut and placed upside down

Measure in centimetres

Bottom filled with water to point where measure starts

17

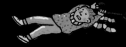

The eye of the hurricane

The *currents of air* in a hurricane spiral upwards to form a rotating circle of wind around a central 'chimney'. This calm centre is called the 'eye'.

SEARCH & FIND

Can you find the satellite?

FIND & SEARCH

Eye

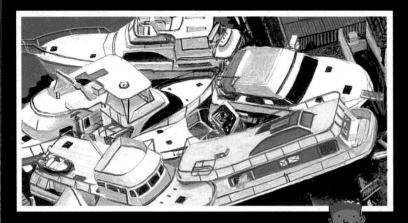

Winds over 300 km/h can cause unimaginable destruction. In 1992, Hurricane Andrew hit an area south of Florida, USA, tearing roofs and walls off houses, smashing trees and cars and piling up these boats like little plastic toys!

 True or false?

Hurricanes are given girls' and boys' names.

Answer: **True**

Atlantic hurricanes are given alternate girls' and boys' names in alphabetical order from the beginning of the season. This makes them easier to identify.

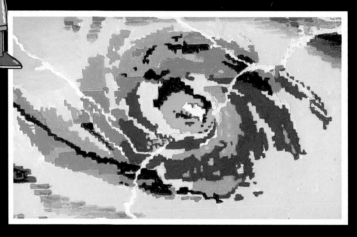

Infra-red pictures from satellites provide colour-coded information about *tropical storms.* Scientists can track their progress and warn people in good time.

Hurricane Andrew caused $20,000,000,000 worth of damage.

Even a solid warship like an aircraft carrier can crumple in a typhoon. This is what happened to *USS Hornet* near Okinawa, Japan, in 1945.

Tropical tantrums

Tropical storms can cause incredible damage. They can whip up huge waves. The highest wave ever measured was 26 m, but the highest ever seen was 34 m. Ships are helpless in such stormy seas.

True or false?

Hurricanes, tropical cyclones and typhoons are all the same thing.

Answer: **True**
Tropical storms are called hurricanes in the Atlantic, cyclones in the Indian Ocean, typhoons in the China Sea and willy-willies in N. Australia.

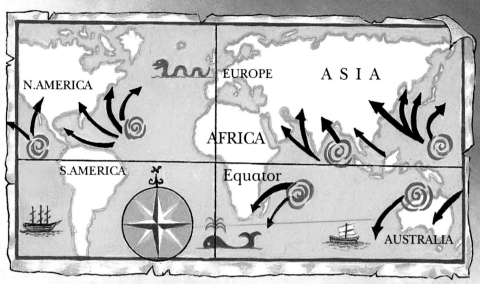

A *storm surge* carried this boat nearly a kilometre inland. Huge waves can surge in ahead of a hurricane, flooding low-lying areas.

Travelling by tornado

Tornadoes are like small, ferocious storms. People, animals and whole houses can be picked up and dropped some distance away. In 1986, thirteen Chinese schoolchildren were carried 19 km by a tornado before being deposited completely unharmed!

A dust devil in the desert is a miniature tornado. Spinning winds whirl sand and dust to heights of between 100–1,000 m.

SEARCH & FIND & FIND SEARCH & FIND SEARCH

Can you find 13 children?

A whirling cloud turns into a waterspout as water is sucked up. It is spectacular, but not terribly dangerous.

A tornado, or 'twister', comes down out of thunder-clouds like an 'elephant's trunk', a spinning funnel of cloud that sucks up dust and soil. The funnel gets tighter and the wind gets faster, up to 650 km/h.

Twister chasers

Not everybody takes shelter in violent weather. The more people understand about tornadoes, the easier it will be to predict when one is coming along. Scientists study tornadoes by following them and putting monitoring equipment in their path to assess their strength.

Tornadoes sometimes appear in pairs. These pairs are called 'sisters'.

An eyewitness described a tornado in 1928: 'The great shaggy end of the funnel hung directly overhead. There was a strong gassy odour. The walls were of rotating clouds with constant flashes of lightning that zigzagged from side to side'.

 True or false?
People can make their own twisters.

Answer: **True**

But not full-size ones! Japanese scientist Tetsuya Fujita studies miniature tornadoes made of dry ice.

 In 24 hrs, 148 tornadoes blew in the southern and mid-west states of the US.

Stripping sandstorms

A sandstorm can easily strip the paint off a car. Loose dust and sand in deserts is whipped up by the wind, flinging millions of stinging grains at every surface. Sand-carrying winds carve desert rocks into strange shapes.

Industrial sand-blasting is used to strip dirt and paint off old buildings to make them look new again.

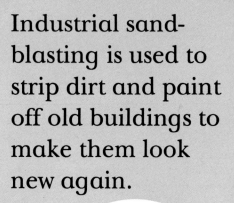

Sand-carved rock found in an American desert

A terrifying 3,000 metre-high dust storm turns the sky dark and sandblasts everything in its path.

There were dust storms in the American mid-west in the 1930s. The rain failed and wind blew the dry soil around. Farmers could grow nothing, so people starved.

True or false?

The Sahara has always been a desert.

Answer: **False**

Climate can change. Cave paintings in the Sahara show that it was once home to all sorts of animals that could only live where there was water and grass.

Forecasts from space

Modern weather forecasts use information gathered from space. Satellites high above the Earth send back pictures of cloud movements. They show where storms are brewing.

This scientist fires a rocket into thunder-clouds. Wires attached to the rocket trigger a charge of lightning.

Weather balloons, called radiosondes, can record and transmit weather conditions as they travel upwards.

Weather stations all over the world take temperature, wind, rain and *air pressure* readings and feed them into computers.

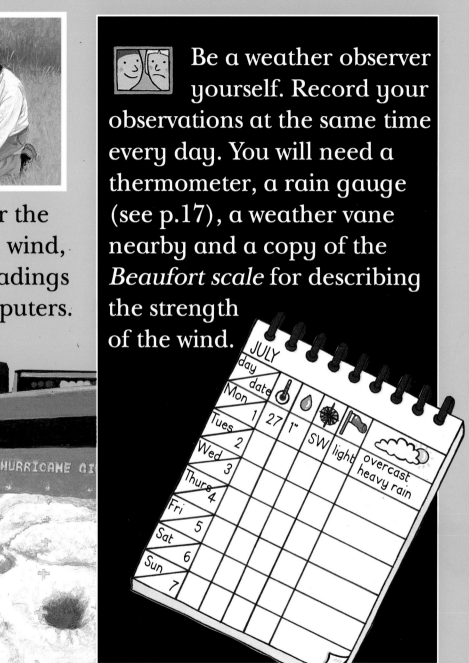

Be a weather observer yourself. Record your observations at the same time every day. You will need a thermometer, a rain gauge (see p.17), a weather vane nearby and a copy of the *Beaufort scale* for describing the strength of the wind.

JULY

day	date	🌡	💧	✳	🚩	☁
Mon	1	27	1"		SW light	overcast heavy rain
Tues	2					
Wed	3					
Thurs	4					
Fri	5					
Sat	6					
Sun	7					

Glossary

Air pressure
The weight of the air pressing down on the land. High pressure usually means settled weather and low pressure usually means bad weather.

Avalanche
Rush of snow down a mountainside.

Beaufort scale
An illustrated scale measuring the force of the wind from calm to hurricane.

Climate
The sort of weather a particular place has come to expect over a long time.

Condensation
Happens when air cools and a gas, such as water vapour, is changed to form droplets of liquid. Clouds are made this way with droplets of water.

Currents of air
Streams of moving air.

Evaporation
This happens when a liquid, such as water, is heated and turns into a gas which rises into the air.

Hailstones
Pieces of ice, formed in thunderclouds, that fall to the ground, often in warm weather.

Infra-red

Satellites can use infra-red
rays to show the different heat
patterns as pictures – clouds
show up as bright (cold) and
deserts as dark (hot).

Storm surge

Waves blown before the wind
which can cause flooding,
especially if forced through a
narrow channel.

Monsoon

The name of
the south-
westerly wind
that brings
heavy rain to
parts of Asia in
the summer; also
the name given to the rainy
season in those places.

Tropical storms

Violent storms that develop
in the hot (over 27° C)
moist air above warm seas
near the Equator in
summer and autumn.

Static electricity

Electricity that isn't flowing in
a current. It builds up from
friction (such as when you rub
a balloon or stroke a cat), or
from lots of activity in a cloud.

Index